Werewolves, ghosts, and vampires too,
with spiders crawling slowly in their hair.

Except for one small zombie boy, who seemed to be afraid.

The zombie boy, who was named Zack, was scared of something you're probably not.

He was frightened that the other kids, would laugh at his farts that smelled a lot.

In the very first class of the day,
the kids all learned to howl,
but Zack could only make his fart,
sound like a hooting owl.

The kids all rolled about and laughed at the really strange and funny noise, but Zack wished he could howl just like the other girls and boys.

But when he tooted as he ran,
bats dropped from the sky and cried.

Since he thought they'd laugh at him,
he ran off, extra, super fast.

One wore a sheet, with eye holes cut, and one was painted green.

But then came something even worse:
a smell that curled his hair.

"We can't believe it, that was great!
We knew that you were cool!
By scaring kids on Halloween,
you're now the best in school!"

Dear reader,

Thank you so much for purchasing and reading this book. It would mean the world to me as an author if you shared your impressions. Please take two minutes to share your review on Amazon with the millions of parents and children (and me!) who are waiting for your valued feedback.

Yours truly,
Tom

Made in United States
North Haven, CT
11 October 2023